The Peculiar Past in the
MIDDLE AGES

by Charis Mather

BEARPORT
PUBLISHING

Minneapolis, Minnesota

Credits

All images are courtesy of Shutterstock.com, unless otherwise specified. With thanks to Getty Images, Thinkstock Photo, and iStockphoto.

Cover – Macrovector, ONYXprj, NotionPic, Nsit, korinoxe, Perfect_kebab. 4–5 – English: Dietrich Reimer, Public domain, via Wikimedia Commons, Leo von Klenze, Public domain, via Wikimedia Commons, vklikov, photo by Grant Mitchell, CC BY 2.0 <https://creativecommons. org/licenses/by/2.0>, via Wikimedia Commons, lemono, kamellys. 6–7 – Vectorfair, Walter Crane, Public domain, via Wikimedia Commons, See U in History, Edouard-Joseph Dantan, Public domain, via Wikimedia Commons, VasyaV, AnonymousUnknown author, Public domain, via Wikimedia Commons, VIATOR IMPERI from HISPANIA, CC BY-SA 2.0 <https:// creativecommons.org/licenses/by-sa/2.0>, via Wikimedia Commons, Maquiladora. 8–9 – R. Lemieszek, elmm, Palazzo Massimo alle Terme, CC BY 2.5 <https://creativecommons.org/ licenses/by/2.5>, via Wikimedia Commons, VasyaV, rizki dian pratama, HappyPictures. 10–11 – Sidhe, oxanaart, Georges Rochegrosse, Public domain, via Wikimedia Commons, Luc-Olivier Merson, Public domain, via Wikimedia Commons. 12–13 – Maso Finiguerra, Public domain, via Wikimedia Commons, Pranch, Top Vector Studio, muratart. 14–15 – Los Angeles County Museum of Art, Public domain, via Wikimedia Commons, Crescenzio Onofri, Public domain, via Wikimedia Commons, Chatree Puksri, Olesia Barhii, Claudia Pylinskaya. 16–17 – Lev Paraskevopoulos, Nicolas-André Monsiau (1754–1837), Public domain, via Wikimedia Commons, Macrovector, delcarmat, Gilmanshin. 18–19 – Apsaras, dominique landau, Andrii Bezvershenko, Nsit, A.B.G., Hoika Mikhail, grmarc. 20–21 – Abraham Janssens I, Public domain, via Wikimedia Commons, serato, GoodFocused, Jean-Léon Gérôme, Public domain, via Wikimedia Commons, Friedrich Georg Weitsch, Public domain, via Wikimedia Commons, Artmim. 22–23 – Henryk Siemiradzki, Public domain, via Wikimedia Commons, Sabelskaya, HappyPictures, Lefteris Papaulakis, NotionPic, ONYXprj, See page for author, CC BY 4.0 <https://creativecommons.org/licenses/by/4.0>, via Wikimedia Commons. 24–25 – M Selcuk Oner, NotionPic, Pong Wira, Ansis Klucis, Wellcome Images, CC BY 4.0 <https:// creativecommons.org/licenses/by/4.0>, via Wikimedia Commons, Photo: Alinari, CC0, via Wikimedia Commons, VectorShow. 26–27 – Unknown man, Internet Archive Book Images, No restrictions, via Wikimedia Commons, Viacheslav Lopatin, Jona Lendering, CC0, via Wikimedia Commons, Evgeniya Mokeeva. 28–29 – tan_tan, Eroshka, ABB Photo, NotionPic, anka77. 30 – Nathan Holland.

Bearport Publishing Company Product Development Team

President: Jen Jenson; Director of Product Development: Spencer Brinker; Managing Editor: Allison Juda; Associate Editor: Naomi Reich; Associate Editor: Tiana Tran; Art Director: Colin O'Dea; Designer: Elena Klinkner; Designer: Kayla Eggert; Product Development Assistant: Owen Hamlin

Library of Congress Cataloging-in-Publication Data is available at www.loc.gov or upon request from the publisher.

ISBN: 979-8-88916-477-7 (hardcover)
ISBN: 979-8-88916-482-1 (paperback)
ISBN: 979-8-88916-486-9 (ebook)

For more information, write to Bearport Publishing, 5357 Penn Avenue South, Minneapolis, MN 55419.

CONTENTS

Strange Time to Be Alive 4

Peculiar People 6

Wealthy and Wacky 8

Dirty Tricks and Nasty Kicks 10

Spoilsports and Painful Punishments 12

Terrible Trials. 14

What's That Smell? 16

Kind of Clean 18

Rats, Fleas, and Deadly Disease. 20

Bloody Barbers 22

Fancy Fighters 24

Conflict at the Castle 26

Bizarre Battles 28

Seriously Strange. 30

Glossary. 31

Index. 32

Read More 32

Learn More Online. 32

STRANGE TIME TO BE ALIVE

Most people who lived during the Middle Ages probably did not think that their everyday world was that weird. But there are certainly some things from this peculiar past that are a lot different than how we live today.

The Middle Ages, also called the medieval era, was a period of European history from about 500 to 1500 CE.

Life in the Middle Ages was full of crazy contrasts and extreme experiences.

THE POWER PYRAMID

Medieval life was very different depending on where you fell in the power pyramid. It was all centered around who owned land and who did not.

Kings

Nobles

Knights

Peasants

Kings owned all the land. They were the most powerful people of this age.

Nobles were given large areas of land by the king. In return, they gave him money and soldiers.

Knights were given small areas of land by nobles and fought in the king's army.

Peasants were the poorest and least powerful people. They worked on farmland that belonged to nobles.

Noble

Peasant

PECULIAR PEOPLE

ANIMAL LOVERS AND HATERS

Popes were powerful religious leaders. People thought God gave them the right to make important decisions for everyone. Yet, some of these popes were odd.

Pope Gregory IX

Pope Gregory IX used his power to declare war against cats. He thought the animals were evil and ordered their deaths!

Pope Gregory IX might not have been the biggest fan of animals, but King Henry III of England was. He had his own zoo filled with three lions, an elephant, and a polar bear!

Henry III was only nine years old when he became king.

NO FAIR!

Many knights competed in jousts. These **mock** fights on horseback let them show what powerful fighters they were. Knight William Marshal used to beat his competitors by grabbing their horses' reins and pulling them out of the fight. Smart? Yes. Fair? Not so much.

Part of being a knight meant fighting fairly. Some knights followed this rule better than others.

Peasants had a hard life. When battles broke out, nobles forced them to fight. An English peasant named Wat Tyler was sick of this. He led a **rebellion**. Unfortunately, he was soon stabbed to death by the nobles.

WEALTHY AND WACKY

They say you can't buy good taste. That was definitely true in the Middle Ages!

BEAUTY IS PAIN

Rich people showed off by dressing up in fancy clothes. Pointy-toed shoes called poulaines were all the rage.

Only the rich and powerful could wear poulaines with really long points. Everyone else had to keep theirs to 2 inches (5 cm) or less!

Poulaines

Poulaines might have been trendy, but they were terrible for the toes. The narrow tips squashed people's feet. Poulaine-wearers sometimes tripped over their shoes, fell, and broke bones!

A FEAST FOR THE EYES

Medieval feasts were designed to impress by serving exotic foods. Typical dishes included barbecued otter and hedgehog, porpoise porridge, and fried whale. Some feasts even served roasted peacock—feathers and all!

Sometimes, feast dishes weren't meant to be eaten. Live frog pie was made just to shock guests. When they sliced into it, out hopped some seriously frazzled frogs!

DIRTY TRICKS AND NASTY KICKS

Medieval fun may not have been very . . . well . . . fun.

THE PRANK GARDEN

Friends of Count Robert II of Artois were in for a shock when they were invited to Hesdin Gardens in what is now Belgium. They faced talking animal statues, trick mirrors, and fountains that sprayed water and flour at people who passed by.

WHAT A JOKER!

Court jesters had one job: to make the king laugh. They usually wore silly costumes and told jokes. Some jesters did magic tricks or sang songs. One king even paid a jester to fart on command!

BRUTAL BALL GAMES

The rich nobles were not the only ones to enjoy fun and games. An early version of soccer was popular with the peasants in medieval times. But the sport involved more fighting than footwork.

Two sides would face off, fighting to get a ball across town any way they could. There were very few rules. Punching and kicking was totally allowed. Things often got violent. Can you imagine playing a sport where you are worried about getting stabbed?

SPOILSPORTS AND PAINFUL PUNISHMENTS

King of England Edward III, royal spoilsport

Kings and nobles laid down some strict laws during the Middle Ages. Some of these spoilsports made it illegal for peasants to wear certain clothes, play certain games, or eat meat on some days.

I declare a ham ban!

As silly as some of the rules were, the punishments for breaking the law were not.

JUST HANGING AROUND

For small crimes, such as lying or cheating, people were locked in a pillory. The wood frame would hold rule-breakers in place by the wrists and neck. People walking by would throw rotten food, rocks, or even poop at those locked in the pillory.

Pillory

If you were caught stealing or committing another big crime, the punishment was much worse. You may have a mark burned into your skin or even have your hand, foot, ear, or nose cut off! For murder and other serious crimes, people were hanged.

13

TERRIBLE TRIALS

What an Ordeal!

Sometimes, determining a person's innocence or guilt was worse than the punishment. You would have to go through a test called an **ordeal**.

ORDEAL BY FIRE

For this test, you would hold a hot metal rod.
Innocent: Your burns healed quickly.
Guilty: Your burns did not heal well.

ORDEAL BY WATER

You'd have your hands and feet tied together. Then, you'd get thrown into water.
Innocent: You sank.
Guilty: You floated.

ORDEAL BY COMBAT

Ordeal by combat involved fighting someone.
Innocent: You lived.
Guilty: You died.

I'm not guilty. I'm just a good swimmer!

From popes to pigs, anyone could end up on trial in the Middle Ages.

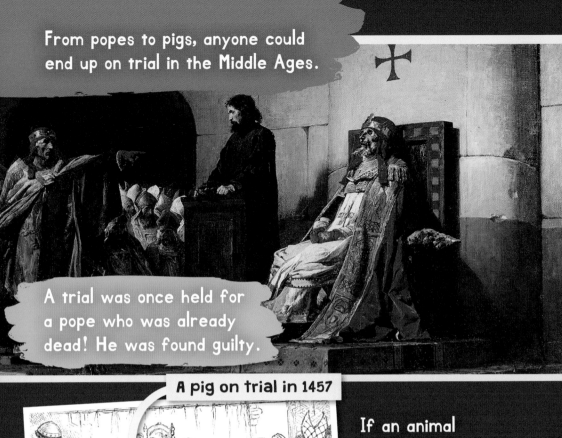

A trial was once held for a pope who was already dead! He was found guilty.

A pig on trial in 1457

If an animal committed a crime, such as biting someone or trampling crops, it could be put on trial. Some animals even had **lawyers.**

Animal trials were held for pigs, rats, dogs, and even insects.

One rooster got in trouble for laying an egg. People were worried that an egg laid by a male chicken would grow into an evil creature. It didn't end well for the bird.

WHAT'S THAT SMELL?

Most medieval people did not have toilets in their homes. Instead, they used public bathrooms or peed and pooped in pots.

HEADS UP!

Some cities had public bathrooms called outhouses. These were just benches with holes cut in them. Some outhouses were built over bridges. Boats passing under the bridge would have to watch out for falling poop. *Gross!*

At home, some people did their business in chamber pots. These buckets would have to be emptied daily.

Some chamber pots were made of clay.

REST IN POO

When poop did not end up in a river, it was often dumped into big holes called cesspits. These pits were not just stinky and gross. They were dangerous, too. Once, a building collapsed over a large cesspit in Erfurt, Germany. At least 60 nobles fell into the poop pit, got stuck, and died. What a gross way to go!

KIND OF CLEAN

When it came to keeping clean, some people put in more effort than others.

THE CLEAN

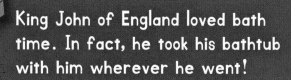

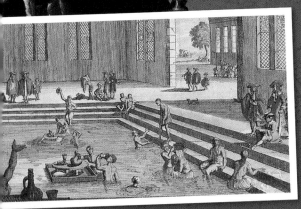

King John of England loved bath time. In fact, he took his bathtub with him wherever he went!

Charlemagne, king of the Franks, liked company when he took a bath. He would bathe in large public pools, sometimes with more than a hundred people.

THE NOT-SO-CLEAN

Queen Isabella of Castile, in what is now Spain, claimed to have bathed only twice in her life!

There were lots of rules that were meant to keep crowded medieval cities clean, but not everyone followed them. What horrible **hazards** would you have had to dodge on the streets?

- Chamber pot puddles
- Animal guts thrown out by butchers
- Animal poop

I'm not paid enough for this.

The dirty job of cleaning this filthy mess up was given to muckrakers.

RATS, FLEAS, AND DEADLY DISEASE

While you might not have enjoyed strolling down stinky medieval streets, rats definitely did. Unfortunately, rats carried fleas, and fleas carried a horrible disease called the **plague**. These fleas passed the disease to humans by biting them.

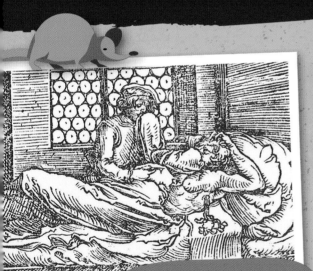

Plague swept through Europe between 1347 and 1351, killing tens of millions of people. This came to be known as the Black Death.

Medieval people did not know that the plague was caused by fleas. Some thought the illness came from pockets of bad air released during earthquakes.

SICKENING SYMPTOMS

Before dying from the plague, many people had some pretty sickening **symptoms**.

- Large sores filled with **pus** on the armpits, neck, and thighs
- Blackening of the skin, especially on the fingers, nose, and toes
- Fever
- Vomiting
- Bleeding from the mouth or nose

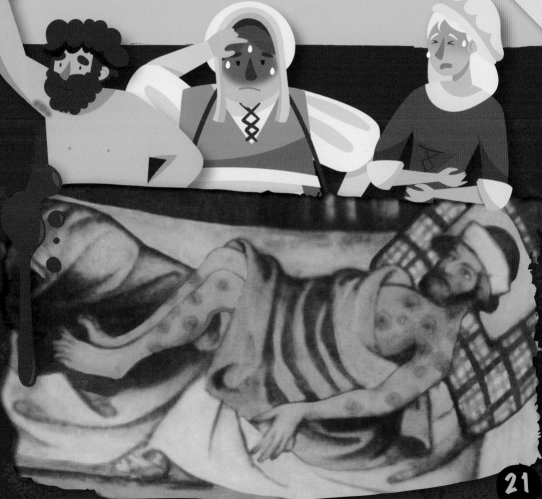

BLOODY BARBERS

If you were sick in the Middle Ages, you'd head to a . . . barber?! Medieval barbers did more than just cut hair. They performed **surgery**, too! But some of their cures were worse than the disease.

TREATMENT FOR BAD BLOOD

Let bloodsucking leeches drink the patient's blood.

Poke holes in the skin to let blood out.

TREATMENT FOR TOOTHACHE

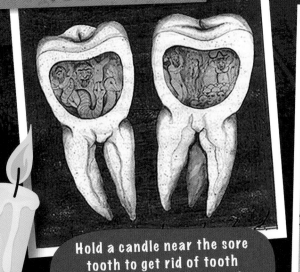

Hold a candle near the sore tooth to get rid of tooth worms. (Thankfully, tooth worms are not a real thing!)

TREATMENT FOR A CRACKED SKULL

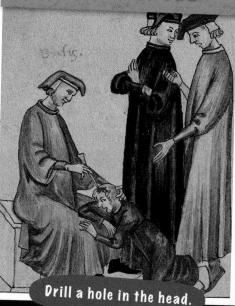

Drill a hole in the head.

22

Doctors **examined** their patients' pee to decide what was making them sick. This included checking its color and smell. Sometimes, they even tasted the pee! *Ew!*

A jar of pee

A pee color chart

SAVED BY THE SURGEON (SORT OF)

In medieval times, doctors still had a lot to learn about the human body. One criminal escaped hanging by agreeing to help surgeons learn more about the body. They cut him open . . . while he was still alive!

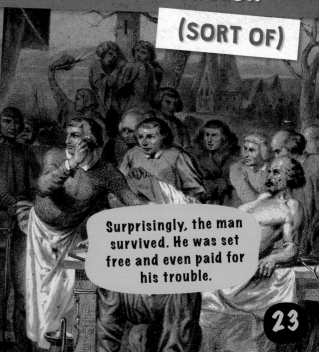

Surprisingly, the man survived. He was set free and even paid for his trouble.

23

FANCY FIGHTERS

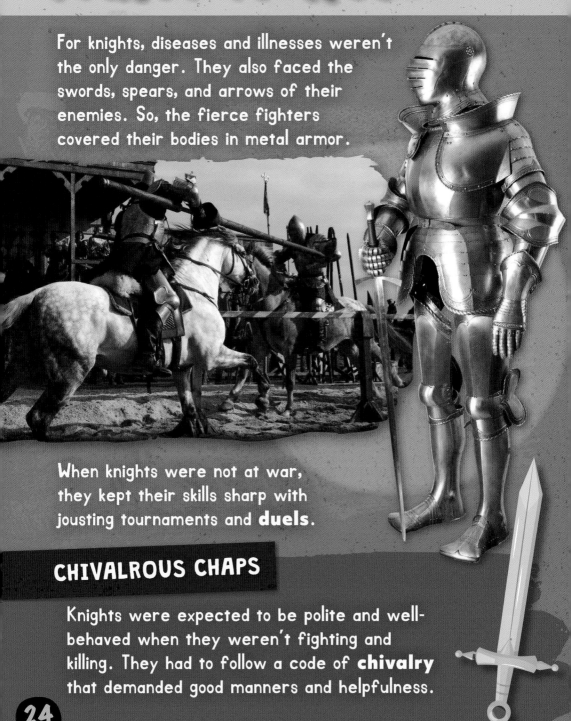

For knights, diseases and illnesses weren't the only danger. They also faced the swords, spears, and arrows of their enemies. So, the fierce fighters covered their bodies in metal armor.

When knights were not at war, they kept their skills sharp with jousting tournaments and **duels**.

CHIVALROUS CHAPS

Knights were expected to be polite and well-behaved when they weren't fighting and killing. They had to follow a code of **chivalry** that demanded good manners and helpfulness.

Most knights were men, but there were a few women who put on armor, too.

I did it for dad!

English noblewoman Agnes Hotot once took the place of her sick father in a jousting tournament. No one knew that she was a woman until after she won the joust.

JOAN OF ARC

Joan of Arc was **17** years old when she convinced King Charles VII of France to let her lead his army. The king agreed and even gave her a suit of armor to wear on the battlefield.

CONFLICT AT THE CASTLE

Knights often fought in and around castles. These mighty buildings were designed to be hard to attack. If enemy armies got across the water-filled **moat**, they still had to find a way over, under, or through the thick stone walls.

Some moats were filled with pee and poop.

Sometimes, attackers surrounded a castle for so long that those inside ran out of food and water. This was called a siege.

During long sieges, people were forced to eat horses, cats, and maybe even leather belts to stay alive.

What **tactics** might help you attack a castle?

- Hurling heavy stones (or dead bodies) using rock launchers.
- Digging tunnels under the castle to make it collapse.
- Climbing the walls with ladders.
- Building tall, moving towers to hide in as you made your way toward the castle.
- Knocking down doors and walls with heavy battering rams.

Medieval Rock Launcher

Those fighting back also had many options.

- Shooting arrows through narrow windows.
- Pushing ladders away from the walls.
- Dropping stones, hot oil, and burning sand or poop on the attackers.

BIZARRE BATTLES

People in the Middle Ages were quick to find reasons to start fights, but some of those reasons were stranger than others.

THE WAR OF THE OAKEN BUCKET

In 1325, a few soldiers from the city of Modena in Italy snuck into Bologna, a neighboring city, and stole an old, wooden bucket. The Bolognese were not happy. They gathered 32,000 soldiers to go to war over the bucket. Somehow, the Modenese beat the much bigger army and kept the bucket as a trophy . . . and then stole another one!

THE SIEGE OF WEINSBERG

After King Conrad III of Germany led the siege of Weinsberg in 1140, he wanted to kill every enemy soldiers inside the castle. But Conrad promised the doomed soldiers that their wives could go free with whatever they could carry. To his surprise, the clever women walked out carrying their husbands. Conrad kept his word, and no one was killed.

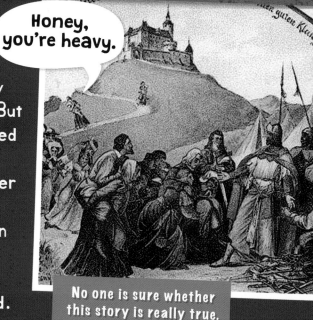

Honey, you're heavy.

No one is sure whether this story is really true.

THE SIEGE OF CHÂTEAU GAILLARD

Prince Phillip II of France won a siege in 1204 in a sneaky—and really stinky—way. His soldiers entered the castle by crawling in the **sewage** pipes and popping up through the toilets.

29

SERIOUSLY STRANGE

Some parts of the Middle Ages were clearly from a peculiar past. From poopy rivers to brutal barbers, the people who lived in the past sure had some terrible tales, surprising stories, and hard-to-believe history!